MW01265238

ISBN: 9798730726444
Independently Published

Turning 65 means you must make a decision about Medicare. You are anxious because it seems so complicated and you're overwhelmed by the tidal wave of advertising. Everyone is telling you what to do, but facts and basic information are hard to find. It seems like the process is designed more for the insurance companies and government than the consumers. Wrong choices and enrollment delays can have a substantial financial impact on your retirement plans. We will simplify the process and guide you to the information you need to make your best decision.

I was raised to respect my elders and provide help whenever possible. This precept, along with helping my brother care for my grandmother and mother before they passed, helped instill a passion for making sure the senior community is never taken advantage of. When the most common phrases I hear are, "Why is this so complicated?", and "Why hasn't anyone ever told me this?", I know that there is a need for balanced information from an ethical agent. This book should help reduce any stress around your Medicare enrollment.

Jon Burgmann

Top 5 Tips to Prepare for Medicare

Medicare Essentials Made Easy

By Jon S Burgmann

Top 5 Tips to Prepare for Medicare

Top 5 Tips to Prepare for Medicare

If you're nearing age 65, you'll soon be faced with making some choices regarding Medicare. In fact, you may have already started to receive phone calls or mail about it, even if it's still years away.

Medicare provides important health insurance protection to millions of seniors and people with disabilities. It can also be very confusing.

Depending on where you live, you could have more than **7,000** different plan options! Choosing the wrong one can cost you money. Worse, you could end up with inadequate coverage when you need it most.

Unfortunately, there's no single, one-size-fits-all answer.

Top 5 Tips to Prepare for Medicare

Trying to navigate the overwhelming amount of Medicare information can feel like entering a dark forest without a map or a flashlight. It can fill the bravest among us with fear and uncertainty. Luckily, there are some things you can do to prepare yourself for your trip through that dark Medicare forest. We're here to be your guide. This document will shine a light on the process and point you toward the path that's best for you and your unique health insurance needs. We've compiled these tips to help you start out on the right foot with confidence.

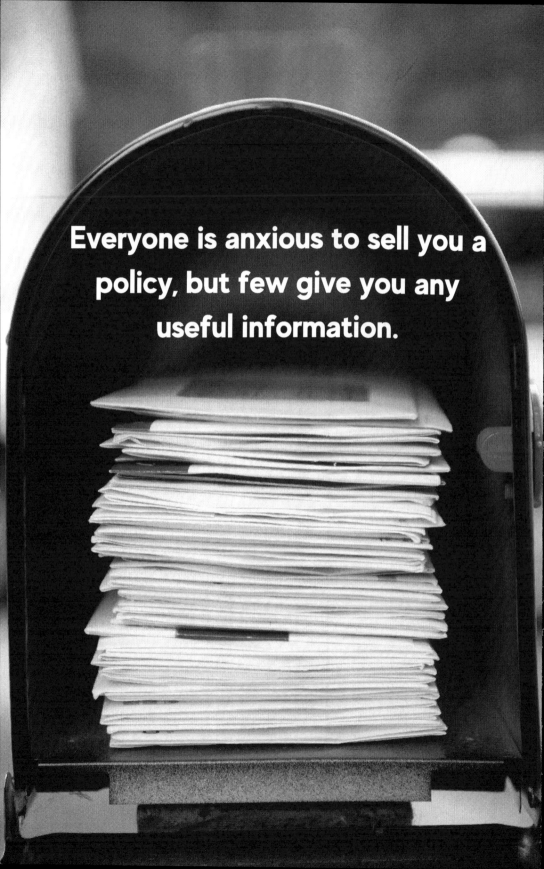

We have clients who have collected boxes of junk mail about Medicare. And even those on the "Do Not Call" list get phone calls all the time. TV ads use celebrities or scare tactics to persuade you. Everyone is anxious to sell you a policy, but few give you any useful information. **Confusing. Intimidating. Overwhelming. Scary.** If any of these words describe how you feel about Medicare, you're not alone. Like most government programs, there are a lot of rules and red tape. You don't need to be an expert—but you'll need help from someone who is.

Once you understand the basics of the Medicare program, you'll feel better about the decisions that are ahead. It's impossible to include all the details of Medicare here, but we'll try to explain the program so it's easier to understand.

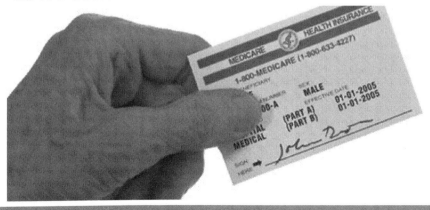

Original Medicare benefits are broken down into Parts A and B. Other parts can be added to create a plan that meets your needs.

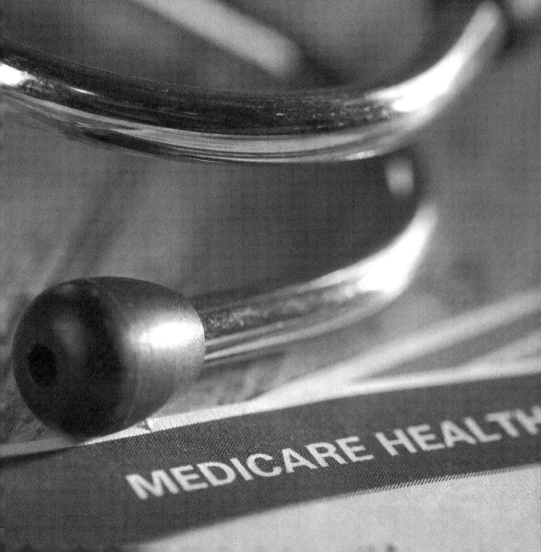

What EXACTLY is Medicare?

Remember all those years of paychecks with payroll tax deductions? The deduction for Medicare is what funds this federal health insurance program. If you worked for a certain amount of time and paid these taxes, you're eligible for Medicare benefits once you turn 65 (or younger with certain disabilities). Original Medicare benefits are broken down into Parts A and B. Other parts can be added to create a plan that meets your needs. **Medicare Part A** covers hospitalization, some nursing care facilities, and hospice care. **Medicare Part B** covers doctor visits, outpatient care, therapy, and medical supplies.

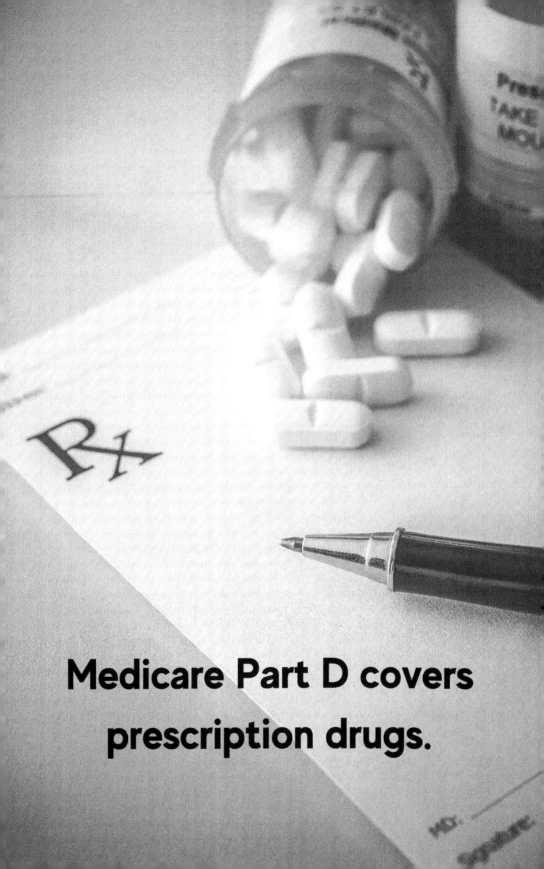

Medicare Part D covers prescription drugs.

What EXACTLY is Medicare?

There's no cost for Part A for most people. As long as you've paid into the fund during your years of work, you're probably covered. If not, you can purchase Part A independently.

Part B and Part D can be added by paying an additional premium. Medicare Supplement or Medigap is additional insurance that can be purchased for an additional fee. It works secondary to Original Medicare and can pay what Medicare leaves behind.

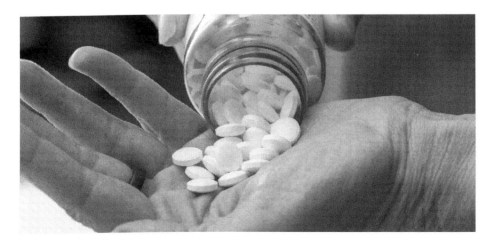

What EXACTLY is Medicare?

Medicare Part C, or Medicare Advantage is an alternative to Original Medicare offered by private insurers. These plans may or may not include Part D, but paying one premium bundles the parts together into one policy. These policies often add some extra benefits such as vision, hearing, or dental coverage.
If that isn't confusing enough, just wait until it's time to choose your particular plan. In Illinois alone, there are over 50 insurance companies that offer up to 10 different Medicare supplemental insurance plans. Depending on where you live, you have 28 different prescription plans and 29 different Medicare Advantage plans to choose from. This adds up to more than 7,000 possible combinations for your coverage!

First, take a deep breath!

If you are feeling overwhelmed with all these choices, you are not alone. It is important to remember that the system was created to ensure that everyone follows the rules. What you decide for your personal situation is not the direct concern of any governmental agency. There's no reason to try to navigate the Medicare forest by yourself. Licensed agents who specialize in Medicare have the knowledge and experience to guide you.

We've just scratched the surface of all there is to know about Medicare. Your next step is to figure out if you're eligible. Then you'll need to decide if it's best to enroll right away or wait. Believe it or not, just because you can enroll, doesn't mean you should. You need the answers to those important questions before you can even think about picking a plan.

Most people think Medicare eligibility begins at 65... but that's only part of the story!

Knowing how important—and confusing—Medicare is, it's tempting to get a head start on figuring out what you need. While research and preplanning make sense for things like a vacation or buying a car, it doesn't work that way with Medicare. First of all, you can't choose plans or do anything until you enroll and receive your assigned Medicare number. This is not the same as your social security number but it's just as important. The problem is, you're not allowed to enroll until close to your 65th birthday.

BEWARE....
Medicare enrollment age
is NOT the same as for
Social Security!

TIP #2:
Timing is Important!

Some people are confused by the fact that you can sign up for social security as early as age 62. Medicare's rules are different and stick to a strict eligibility window surrounding your 65th birthday unless you are receiving Social Security Disability. The window of time that you are eligible to enroll starts three months before the month you turn 65. For example, if your birthday is in September, you can start the enrollment process in June, July, or August. When you enroll during that time frame, your coverage starts on September 1st. (There's an exception if your birthday is on the 1st of the month. In that case, your enrollment in Medicare starts the 1st of the previous month, and your window starts three months before that.)

Your Medicare Initial Enrollment Period (IEP)

If you turn 65 in...

JANUARY
the **October** before
your birthday
— *through* —
the **April** after
your birthday

FEBRUARY
the **November** before
your birthday
— *through* —
the **May** after
your birthday

MARCH
the **December** before
your birthday
— *through* —
the **June** after
your birthday

APRIL
the **January** before
your birthday
— *through* —
the **July** after
your birthday

MAY
the **February** before
your birthday
— *through* —
the **August** after
your birthday

JUNE
the **March** before
your birthday
— *through* —
the **September** after
your birthday

JULY
the **April** before
your birthday
— *through* —
the **October** after
your birthday

AUGUST
the **May** before
your birthday
— *through* —
the **November** after
your birthday

SEPTEMBER
the **June** before
your birthday
— *through* —
the **December** after
your birthday

OCTOBER
the **July** before
your birthday
— *through* —
the **January** after
your birthday

NOVEMBER
the **August** before
your birthday
— *through* —
the **February** after
your birthday

DECEMBER
the **September** before
your birthday
— *through* —
the **March** after
your birthday

Source: Medicare MarketPlace

Researching plans too early is often a waste of time. Medicare plans change frequently, so even looking into your options 6 or 8 months before your birthday is too soon.

Benefits and prices can change by the time your birthday rolls around. The eligibility window stays open another 3 months after your birthday month. In our example of a September birthday, you can enroll in October, November, or December.

Why is it important to enroll during the eligibility window? If you miss it, you need to wait until the General Enrollment Period, unless you are working and covered by your employer's plan. The General Enrollment Period extends from January through March of the following year. More importantly, your benefits will not begin until July 1st!

Enrolling in Medicare is not the same as picking a supplement or advantage plan. That part comes later, so no matter what an advertisement or salesman claims, Medicare enrollment dates are set in stone.

That won't stop them from trying to lock you into an agreement with their company for a plan, so it is important for you to be aware!

Some Medicare sales representativ es will try and lock you into an agreement no matter the timing in order to get a quick sale. This may lock you into a plan that's not the best for you!

If you enroll in the wrong coverage, you might be able to switch in the future, but your options may be limited due to your health history.

Learn more about our local seminars at www.yourtrustedmedicaresource.com

Perhaps you are the type of person who wants to learn about your options and understand the process. That's great and we get it. But instead of studying up on something that's probably going to change, we encourage you to attend one of our classes or seminars. You'll find out more of what you need to know, without making any important decisions too soon.

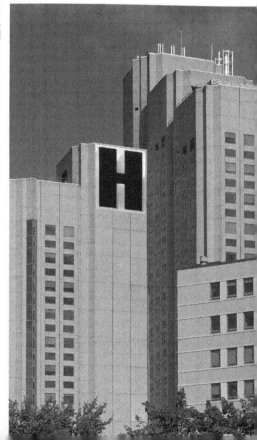

Keep your medical information up to date and have it handy when you're ready to speak to anyone about your Medicare options.

If you like to be proactive, here's something you can do right now: Make a list of all of your current prescriptions and all the doctors you see. Also make note of your preferred hospital(s). You will need all of this information when you pick a plan, so it's a good idea to keep it up to date and have it handy when you're ready to speak to anyone about your Medicare options. Look for the pages in the Appendix to you help you with this.

You don't Have to enroll in Medicare, as long as you or your spouse are still working and part of a group insurance plan.

TIP #3:
You don't have to enroll...
Just because you are eligible!

So, once you turn 65, do you have to go on Medicare?

Actually, you don't, as long as you or your spouse are still working and part of a group insurance plan. In fact, in some cases, it might be smarter to stick with that coverage. It's important to note that **if you do not fit that description exactly, you must enroll in Medicare or risk financial penalties when you finally do enroll.** If you do fall into that category, your decision of whether or not to enroll in Medicare right now should take into account the amount of your current premium, how much you're required to pay out-of-pocket for medical care, and if there are other people (a spouse or children) included in your coverage. Medicare might be the most economical choice for your family, or it might not.

Often, the decision is less about you than about your family members.

TIP #3:
You don't have to enroll...
Just because you are eligible!

Your Medicare enrollment covers you, and only you. If a family member is not eligible for Medicare yet, they could lose their benefits when you quit your insurance plan from work. They may be allowed to stay on the group plan through COBRA, a government act that ensures the continuation of health coverage. The cost is entirely your responsibility, though, without an employer match. Another option is to purchase a policy on the open market and possibly receive a federal subsidy through the Affordable Care Act (ACA) to help pay for it.

Case Study #1:

Mr. K was ready to retire at 65 and go on Medicare, but Mrs. K was only 63 and not eligible yet. She was included in his policy from work and would lose her benefits once he retired. They didn't qualify for an ACA(American Cares Act) subsidy, so the best policy we found for them on the open market would cost her $1086 a month with a $2700 deductible.

They opted to keep her on Mr. K's employer's insurance plan through COBRA, where her premiums were $680 a month instead.

Case Study #2:

Mr. G was 60 years old and still working. Mrs. G was 68, but was still on his group insurance plan. They assumed it was better than having her go on Medicare. It turns out they were paying more than $450 a month just to keep her on the employer's plan. There was also a maximum out-of-pocket cost of $4000 per person. She enrolled in Medicare and received 100% health coverage for less than $300 a month.

Mr. G stayed on his insurance with individual coverage at a lower cost instead of paying a higher price for family member coverage.

TIP #3:
You don't have to enroll...
Just because you are eligible!

While you're dreaming of trips to take and fun things to do with the grandkids when you retire, you can't ignore health insurance coverage. We hate to be the bearer of bad news, but when you transition from a paycheck to social security, your income will go down. Meanwhile, your living expenses will stay the same or go up, and that's even if you stay healthy for decades.

Sadly, retirement for some people means taking a huge financial hit. They simply can't afford to pay for private insurance or a Medicare premium on their retirement budget. If your employer offers a good health plan at a low cost, it might make sense to keep working.

You will want a trusted professional advisor

with the tools to help you figure out what's best for you

TIP #3:
You don't have to enroll...
Just because you are eligible!

So how do you know if Medicare, COBRA, or a group plan are best for you and your family? And can you even afford to retire right now? You're going to have to crunch some numbers to figure it all out and that's no easy task. You will need a trusted professional advisor with the tools to help you sort it out.

But don't trust just anyone with the future of your finances and health coverage.

It's too big of a gamble for you and your family's future. Be sure to read our section on Red Flags. It will help you weed out those who aren't looking out for your best interest.

If you're already receiving social security, you're automatically enrolled in Medicare Part A and Part B, effective the first day of the month you turn 65.

Once you've determined that the time is right for you to go on Medicare, the next step is fairly simple: find out if you're enrolled. If you're already receiving social security, you're automatically enrolled in Medicare Part A and Part B, effective the first day of the month you turn 65. If you're receiving social security disability benefits, it will happen 2 years after that start date.

If you are not getting social security, you need to initiate the enrollment into Medicare on your own.

If you are not getting social security, you need to initiate the enrollment into Medicare on your own. This can be done online at the Social Security Administration website (ssa.gov) or the Medicare website (Medicare.gov). You can also enroll by phone or in person at a Social Security Administration office. Remember, though, to wait until the 3 month (90 day) window before your 65th birthday month. As we all know, the wheels of government agencies turn slowly, so it's best to do this as soon as possible within those 3 months.

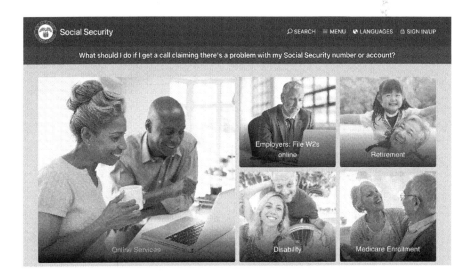

If you're not currently receiving social security, you'll have to pay that premium yourself.

It's important to note that you are allowed to enroll in Medicare and wait until a later date to enroll in social security. If you are collecting social security, your premium for Medicare Part B will be deducted automatically from your monthly benefit. If you're not receiving social security, you'll need to pay that premium yourself.

Let's review!

To enroll in Medicare coverage:

- Determine the eligibility window based on your birth date.
- Decide if Medicare is your best health insurance option at this point in time.
- Find out if you're already enrolled. If not, go through the enrollment process.

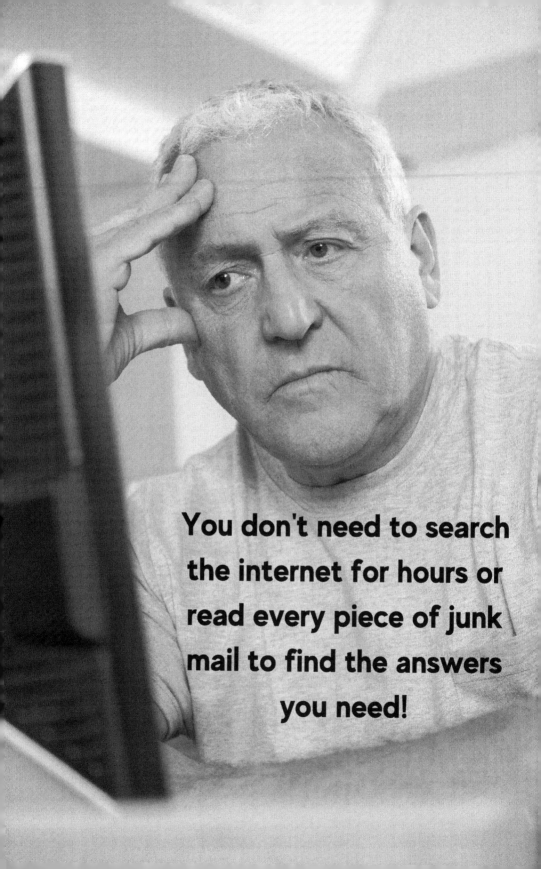

Now comes the tricky part—analyzing your situation and choosing the best plan out of more than 7,000 possible combinations.

Are you prepared to search the internet or read every piece of junk mail to find the answer?

Will you follow the advice of a celebrity on TV?

The stakes are high. The decisions made at this point can impact your health care options and financial wellbeing—and that of your family—for years to come. It's time to tune out the robocalls, junk mail, and TV commercials and get the help of a local, licensed, experienced professional you can trust.

Call center sales professionals may not have the expertise YOU need!

In one of our recent seminars, Mrs. B told the story of her experience with another insurance agent. She had trouble getting anyone to call her back, and when they finally did, she couldn't get any straight answers.

Frustrated, she finally called the company directly. Since she had an idea of the plan she wanted, Mrs. B went ahead and enrolled with the salesperson who answered the phone.

The salesperson was friendly and probably meant well, but it wasn't her job to ask any questions or discuss Mrs B's needs or retirement plans. We reviewed her situation and discovered a different plan that would have been a much better choice for Mrs. B.

Without the knowledge and expertise of a trusted advisor, you may end up with a plan that doesn't provide you the coverage you need at a cost you cannot afford!

Unfortunately, Mrs. B's story is common. People sometimes decide to trust someone who isn't knowledgeable about Medicare, who doesn't ask the right questions, or simply is trying to sell a specific plan.

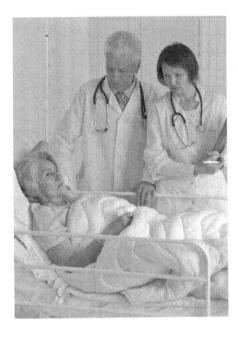

Or, they go to a website themselves and attempt to make sense of all the information. Just like doing your own taxes or writing a will, you can sign up for your supplement or advantage plan yourself, but should you?

Consider how much time, effort, and headaches it will take. Then add in the consequences of picking a plan that leaves you underinsured and unprotected in the event of a serious illness or injury.

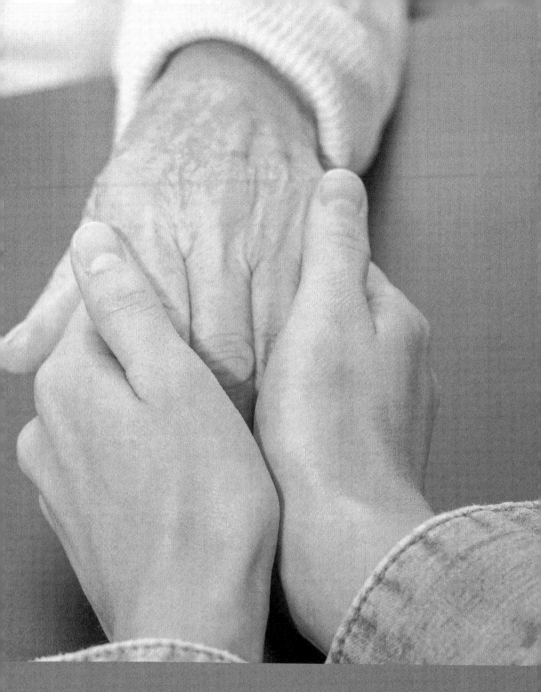

Whether you work with an agency, go straight to an insurance company, or enroll by yourself on the Medicare website, your premiums will be exactly the same.

There's a simpler and safer solution. If you already have an agent, they have hopefully already shared this information with you. If not, we'd be happy to become your trusted advisor and start the conversation about how best to protect your future. The best part? Whether you work with an agency like the Burgmann Insurance Group, go straight to an insurance company, or enroll by yourself on the Medicare website, your premiums will be exactly the same.

Burgmann
Insurance
Group

Yourtrustedmedicaresource.com

Customer Ser

Excellent ☑

Very good ☐

Good ☐

Average ☐

Poor ☐

So what's the difference?

With a local, respected agent like Jon Burgmann, you'll get individual attention in finding the perfect set of benefits for you at the best cost. Plus, you'll have superior customer service any time you need it. You won't get that from a big insurance company, and certainly not from the U.S. Department of Health and Human Services that oversees Medicare.

Our five tips will hopefully help you gain clarity about Medicare and the enrollment process. However, there are other dangers for which you need to be prepared.

BEWARE of these red flags!

Not only are Medicare choices complicated and overwhelming, there are plenty of companies out there that are willing to take advantage of your confusion. Others simply don't have the experience or resources needed to navigate the Medicare forest.

The following red flags are signs of someone who is not looking out for you.

Most robocalls, junk mail, and TV ads have one goal—to make a quick sale.

One Size DOES NOT Fit All.

Your situation is unique, and so is your Medicare solution. Don't pick a plan simply because it's what a friend or family member chose. It might work great for them, but may not be best for you.

Ignore "Act Now!" Tactics.

Most robocalls, junk mail, and TV ads have one goal—to make a quick sale. They'll try to fill you with a false sense of urgency, even if your enrollment window is years away. It's a high-pressure sales tactic meant to fill you with anxiety. Remember that everything can change if you research plans too soon. Don't jump into anything until you're sure it's right for you, and don't ever feel pressured into buying anything you don't understand or aren't comfortable with.

ATM

Beware of licensed agents requiring payment for meeting with them.

Don't Pay a Fee.

You should never have to pay a licensed agent for their Medicare advice—they are paid by the insurance companies they represent. Beware of any advisor charging a fee to review your options or help you pick a plan. Agents who charge a "meeting fee" or "consultation fee" may not be certified to sell the products they're suggesting and are instead trying to get you to pay for their time. We have encountered people who have been charged for a review, only to discover they didn't need to change anything about their current plan. Why should you pay for that?

Beware of "Captive" Agents.

A general agent can contract with most insurance companies, but a captive agent can only sell products from a specific insurance company. They will steer you toward their company's policies, giving you a small portion of the options available to choose from.

There are Limits to Free Advice.

There are grant-funded, non-profit organizations that will offer free advice. They can be helpful in answering questions about Medicare. However, they are typically not licensed insurance agents and should not be recommending which products you should take. You will have no recourse if they make a mistake in their advice, and no one to call for follow-up customer service.

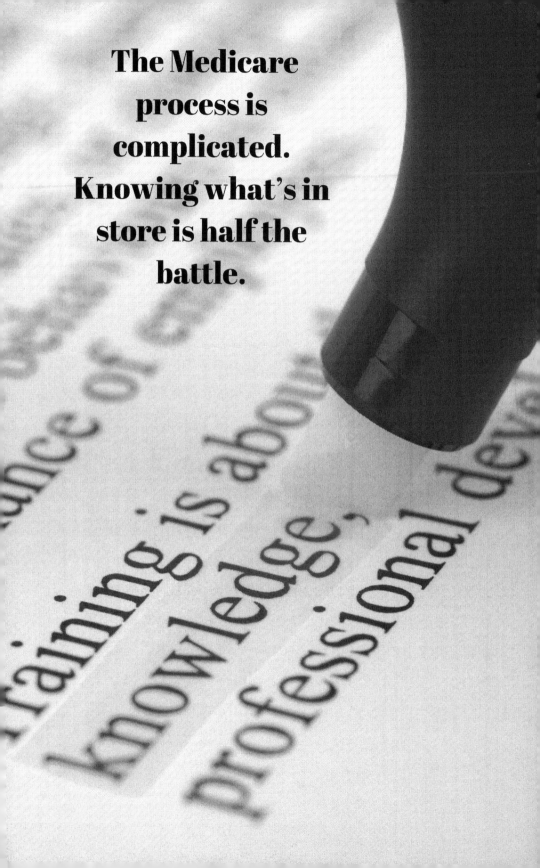

The Medicare
process is
complicated.
Knowing what's in
store is half the
battle.

We know we've thrown a lot of information at you!

We've tried our best to make it easy to understand. When it's time to start planning your Medicare journey, keep our 5 tips in mind:

1. <u>Understand the Medicare Program</u>. It's complicated, knowing what's in store is half the battle.
2. <u>Timing is Important</u>. Medicare timelines are set in stone. Know yours and don't miss it.
3. <u>You Don't Have to Enroll Just Because You're Eligible</u>. Get help to determine if Medicare is the right choice, right now, for you and your family.
4. <u>Ready to Enroll? Follow the Steps—In the Right Order</u>. If Medicare is the best (or only) way to go, enroll and obtain your Medicare number.
5. <u>Get Help Choosing Your Plan</u>. Remember that there are more than 7,000 possible options. Connect with a trusted advisor to reduce your stress and anxiety.

With more than 7,000 possible Medicare options, is this something you want to tackle on your own? Connect with a trusted advisor to reduce your stress and anxiety. If you don't have one, call us. We are always happy to help.

Keep these 5 key tips in mind as you prepare for Medicare. Remember that their order is important too, but don't be embarrassed to ask for help if it all makes you feel stressed and confused. That's perfectly natural. The good news is that you don't have to figure it all out on your own. We highly recommend seeking the help of an experienced Medicare insurance professional instead of going it alone. You'll be much more confident once you find someone you can trust to guide you through the decision process. We specialize in doing just that.

Worrying about your wellbeing and how you'll pay for medical care can stand in the way of the happy retirement you envision for yourself.

Burgmann Insurance Group
Your Trusted Medicare Source

Uncertainty is scary. Fear of failing health, your finances, and your family's future can all keep you up at night. As you get older, making the right decisions about your health care and insurance decisions is more important, and more stressful, than ever. Worrying about your wellbeing and how you'll pay for medical care can stand in the way of the happy retirement you envision for yourself.

What are your dreams for retirement? Maybe you want to travel, explore new hobbies, or just spend more time with your grandchildren. Whatever your future plans happen to be, they'll be that much sweeter knowing your health insurance decisions are taken care of. You owe it to yourself—and your loved ones—to make sure

your health and financial security are squared away so you can make those dreams happen.

Burgmann Insurance Group
Your Trusted Medicare Source

Start your journey with Burgmann Insurance Group as your guide. We offer unbiased Medicare advice that fits your goals, and never charge for consultations. We'll help you find your way through the Medicare maze by shining a light on the best path for you, and we'll stick with you every step of the way.

For straight answers to all your Medicare questions, contact the Burgmann Insurance Group at
618-206-2623,
or email Medicare@Burgmanninsgroup.com.

Over the last 10 years Jon has heard almost every Medicare question out there. But, hearing stories about unethical agents and elder abuse, along with his experience of helping to care for both his grandmother and mother drives his passion for protecting the senior community. Today he works with the Elder Justice Council of St. Clair County to raise awareness of issues and scams related to elder abuse. He also provides free Medicare seminars and classes to give everyone the educational tools they need to make the best decisions that are right for them.

"I attended one of Jon's Medicare Question and Answer sessions at our local library. It wasn't a sales pitch. He simply gave us information and answered our questions. I later called him back and set up an appointment to select a supplement. He met with us, showed us a myriad of choices and let us choose the plan we felt comfortable with, and signed us up. I would recommend him to anybody. He showed a passion for helping people navigate Medicare."
~Jeff and Jane Johnson

"Jon was personable and very clear with his presentation. I have worked in a world of corporate issues all my life and understand what motivates people. Jon is motivated by serving his clients. Thank you Jon!"~Roger Kriegel

Hopefully, since you have made it this far, you are feeling less overwhelmed by the whole Medicare process. Let's try and reduce that stress even further by compiling some information you can use when you are meeting with your trusted Medicare agent and deciding on your next step.

Name:_____

Address:_____

City:_____

State:_____ Zip:_____

Phone #:_____

Your DOB:_____

Your Medicare #:_____

Married? Y/N

Spouse Name:_____

Spouse DOB:_____

Spouse's Medicare #:

_____

Your Current Insurance Plan:

_____

How much of your monthly premium is for you?_____

How much of your monthly premium is for your spouse?

_____

Preferred Contact Method:

Phone Text Email Mail

Your current insurance Policy Number:_____

Is anyone else covered under your insurance? Y / N

If so, please list their names:_____

_____

If you enroll in Medicare, will your spouse lose coverage? Y / N

What is your current insurance deductible & Max out of pocket?

_____

How much will your spouse pay on Cobra? (ask your HR Dept.)

_____

 Burgmann Insurance Group   (618) 206-2623   info@burgmanninsgroup.com
yourtrustedmedicaresource.com

Knowing your thoughts about retirement will help us find the most appropriate Health Insurance plan for your situation.

What is the annual Household income expected to be when you retire?_____

What are your biggest concerns about retirement? These are the things that keep you up at night. (circle all that apply)
cash flow, investment stability, longevity, family, healthcare costs, Other(list below)

_____
_____
_____
_____
_____
_____
_____

What activities are you thinking of doing in retirement that are different from how you currently live? Will you travel or maybe become snowbirds, etc.?

_____
_____
_____
_____
_____

Now let's hear about your Medicare Concerns.

What are your fears or concerns about enrolling with, or being on Medicare? What have you heard that worries you? Are you more concerned about the price, or your choice of doctors, etc.)

_____

_____

_____

Please rank the importance of the following items as they relate to your health insurance needs and wants: (1=not important, 5=must have)

Choice of Doctors _____ 1 2 3 4 5

No/Low Premium _____ 1 2 3 4 5

Vision Plan _____ 1 2 3 4 5

Dental Plan _____ 1 2 3 4 5

Hearing Plan _____ 1 2 3 4 5

Paid Meals _____ 1 2 3 4 5

Paid Travel to/from Dr Appts _____ 1 2 3 4 5

OTC Meds & Supplies Provided _____ 1 2 3 4 5

Home Health Care _____ 1 2 3 4 5

Prepay for your medical care _____ 1 2 3 4 5

Ease of use _____ 1 2 3 4 5

No Copays _____ 1 2 3 4 5

Pay as You Go for medical care _____ 1 2 3 4 5

Paid Gym Membership _____ 1 2 3 4 5

Other? _____

Remember, there are no plans where everything is included. Each benefit has a cost. We'll help you pick the best options for your situation.

Burgmann Insurance Group

(618) 206-2623   info@burgmanninsgroup.com

yourtrustedmedicaresource.com

Prescription List

Your ability to qualify for different plans will be based on your current health. All plans will require this information. Please list all of your current prescriptions. Do not include over the counter medicines or supplements. Don't forget inhalers, infusions, or injection medications.

Prescription Name	Dosage	Frequency

1_____

2_____

3_____

4_____

5_____

6_____

7_____

8_____

9_____

10_____

11_____

12_____

13_____

14_____

15_____

16_____

17_____

18_____

19_____

20_____

Must Haves

Please list any doctors or hospitals that you want to make sure are included in the health insurance plan you select. These are the doctors and medical centers that you refuse to part with. If you saw a doctor once, three years ago, don't include them.

Use the following space for taking notes or additional questions you may have.

Burgmann Insurance Group

(618) 206-2623   info@burgmanninsgroup.com

yourtrustedmedicaresource.com